The Girl From Yesterday

The Girl From Yesterday

Poems by June Sylvester Saraceno

Cherry Grove Collections

© 2020 by June Sylvester Saraceno

Published by Cherry Grove Collections

P.O. Box 541106

Cincinnati, OH 45254-1106

ISBN: 978-1-62549-334-7

Poetry Editor: Kevin Walzer

Business Editor: Lori Jareo

Visit us on the web at www.cherry-grove.com

Acknowledgements

Grateful acknowledgement goes to the editors of journals and anthologies where these poems, or earlier versions of them, were first published.

Adirondack Review: "County Cork"

Big Muddy: "Brood" "Firewood and Brimstone" and "Prodigal Birthright"

Bridge Eight Magazine: "Rooftops"

Fiction Week Literary Review: "Outside the Metro" (previously titled "I Should Have Brought More Gifts")

Ithaca Lit: "Forgive Me"

Kokanee: "Edge of Morning," "Personal Effects," and "Salvage" (previously titled "Seafaring")

Lady Liberty Lit: "Hair Fable" and "Late Morning in Bed"

Poetry South: "Voice Lessons"

Tar River Poetry: "Riding a Bike in Marnay at Dusk" and "Things Left Out in the Rain"

Tiferet: "Window" and "Legacy" (previously titled "Family History")

Thin Air Magazine: "Unsung Communion" (previously titled "Unsung Mass")

Up the Staircase Quarterly: "Night Currents"

Zo Magazine: "Lady in Green and Gold"

Heartfelt thanks to Gayle Brandeis, Rick Campbell, Robin Griffin, and Brian Turner for expert editing advice, and generous support along the way. Deep appreciation to Aydelette Isgar for artistic vision and technical hoodoo. My gratitude for the residency at Maison Verte in Marnay-sur-Seine, France, where many of these poems first emerged. Many thanks to Kevin Walzer and Lori Jareo at WordTech Communications for publishing this collection.

"The people of this world are moving into the next, and with them their hours and the ink of their ability to make thought."

Carolyn Forché *Nocturne, an elegy (Blue Hour)*

For Dylan, my sun and stars

Table of Contents

III

I

Legacy

I loved the dirt under my nails,

summer-calloused feet.

I'm grateful you left me feral

to roam the fields and woods,

to sink my hands in ochre earth.

I hated the belt—raising

crimson welts on my legs.

Tongue lashings. Church.

Church most of all—

the long drone of it,

leaving sunshine and grass

waiting outside.

Now, my own child is grown,

and I gave him no church,

except my love. Was it enough?

How could it ever be?

The only home for him

to inherit is our shared memories:

A wave knocked us down,

another brought us

back to shore. Look to the sea.

Go there.

Window

The window fills with gardenia bloom in evening.

The humid air, my sister's voice, this window

I raise and lower across elastic time.

Some days the window is out of reach.

I have to climb the trellis that rose to yesterday

and disappeared in winter. I

build steps out of snow and pack them down

with stomping, with *sturm und drang*, with salt.

It's worth the effort. Every effort.

Though who knows what the window will let in or out?

Sometimes a slight crack and angry voices engulf

the space in flames. Always somewhere a burning roof.

Sometimes the corn stalks arc so high that boys climb

them to carve their initials in the flesh of the moon.

Sometimes the window wells with salt spray from an ocean

that buoys and baptizes, but also serves up jellyfish and trash.

I look for the family portrait there, moving frames –

a lullaby slips out, a dime locket, cootie catchers,

a fish hanging from the lightbulb, duck quack,

peed-in underpants stuffed behind a freezer,

mittens and carpet burns, a clue in a clock tower,

backwards braille of names knifed into the sill,

a diary with a broken lock, galoshes, smoke,

a revival tent of dire prophecies, lightening bugs,

ticks, scabs, the hanged man, angels glinting,

a sack of pecans, a rusted tractor, a fly swatter.

It's only a first story window.

It has more stories than stars.

If I don't open it,

I'll never get out.

Brood

Our breed was a brooding type,

menfolk in barns and garages, silent,

thick fingers turning tools.

Those hands could snap a shoulder

back in place, or drown a litter

of unwanted pups. They did

what had to be done, without a fuss.

Summer brought a bounty of small

skeletons, surfacing from shallow digs

in the piney woods.

Mothers, captive in their kitchens,

call children in when the evening

star brightens and bats begin to flit.

Call children in to supper, in for the night.

Then recall the lost ones, the nameless ones,

swallow hard, blink them back to shadow.

Turned gruff, these mothers stand

what they can, what they must,

and command: *don't track in mud.*

They knew the patch of earth allotted,

the garden toil, the final bed where

they would rest, marked as well

as times allowed. Wary folk,

dead set against raising false hope,

they warned in word and deed

bloodlines map existence.

We, their sullen children,

even if we could, would not resist

entirely, the stubborn pull

our dirt-lined palms predicted.

Even were we able to break

Earth's gravity, to rise like Venus,

bright in the gathering dark, put distance

between us, who would choose

to quench that old smoldering fire,

banked deep in the blood?

Who would choose to leave?

Firewood and Brimstone

for my father, the preacher

I see you in the distance,

in the rise and fall of your chainsaw

through the felled tree, your broad plaid back

straining under noon-day heavens,

the steady lull and crescendo of providing firewood.

Icy-eyed surveyor,

discontent furrowed in your brow.

Your hands would not be idle,

with those long fingers, you might have played

piano, but the brogans on your feet

pointed to the ploughshare, hard walking

on this narrow path.

What was it that God said to you?

His word a stone slab around your neck.

And me, flint striking, striking to find

beneath the cold, what beat at the heart.

You stood your ground, unmoved,

though sometimes scanning the trees,

you must have heard the mingled mockingbird,

but refused the cross-veined time hatched there.

What was this call from God?

More lightning than light, it seems,

more thunder than steady pulse of rain.

Was it hard tilling such rocky soil,

knowing the rod of so many generations,

the monumental weight of forbearers?

I see you, man of sorrow, yellowing

in a photograph that flattens

your dimensions in my hands. I cannot hear

or know what God said to you, or how

you came to be rendered up to Caesar's gate

with so much iron, but no key forged of it.

Unsung Communion

Here is the cart without the push, laden

heavy as the holy spirit, untongued,

tire not yet inspired into wheel.

Here a monarch of airy tides awaits

an Ariel both bound and freed in the unspoken

tree, silent bark falling, falling away.

Here untasted bread waits to be wafer

transubstantiated moment of yeast, of yearn

of flesh and spirit, body and soul.

Speak to me. Have you forgotten?

The blue throat of sky, guttural and distant.

Speak to me. Have you forgotten?

The earth rises in wails underfoot.

Speak to me. Have you forgotten?

The stony pulse, cradle song, the rocking.

Overdue Elegy for Granddaddy Gray

I didn't see you go. You might have

just wandered off to the garden,

or drifted off like smoke curling from a chimney.

The melted nougat of hidden candy,

your last gift.

You were brief in my life—

tricycle days, before school

or learning to tie shoelaces.

You were crew-cut-white, sea-eyed,

grizzle-chinned, superman big.

We recited nightly,

"Now I lay me down to sleep…"

You scratched my cheek with yours,

then warbled a song about the moon

through the leaves of the old oak tree,

shining on the ones we love.

I never said goodbye, unaware

you wouldn't reappear, not at bedtime,

not even at Christmas.

This is it, then. The farewell so long overdue,

it condenses in the air and vanishes

in this cold attic, absent you.

Prodigal Birthright

My mother wanted me to be happy which to her meant satisfied, so she discouraged too much hope, too much wanting. She said *you're too young for your wants to hurt you*. I never understood those words, as if they arrived in a language that traveled across the seas with her desperate ancestors. So much about her I didn't understand. But I knew she wanted me to be happy, which to her was the absence of misery. To any wish bubbling from my mouth, she repeated *I wouldn't count on it*. *I wouldn't count on it* the kitchen sink recited, the coffee pot refrained. Sometimes a *we'll see* slipped out to counter the refrain, making me bite my bottom lip to stop a smile too wide. *We'll see* was a crack in the door that might lead somewhere. When I was very small, she let me brush out her long hair, freed from its twists and pins. I brushed, she hummed. I could feel her drift away from wishes for my happiness and into a moment of her own content, her own being. She liked her scalp rubbed. My hands knew power then, and I stood over her. We sorted ourselves, like dark colors and light, to be washed separately. I was happy with my fingers in her hair but I had no word for it. It sounded like her humming. It felt like her thick locks in my hands. She was protective. Maybe I would be Mary in the Christmas play? *Don't count on it.*

Maybe that boy liked me back? Don't count on it. So few things could be counted on, the ones that could were weighted with inevitability, an apron filled with clothes pins, diminishing returns. When I struck out, I struck hard. Ran fast. Swallowed the sky. Meteor burning through the night, my leaving. I consumed the fat meat, the gristle, the bone, the bloody juice of it all. But she had blessed me already. So that when I returned, and she was very small folding into herself, I knew not to hope too hard. In the end, I wished her happiness, the absence of suffering. I wanted to wish her joy, but I knew that we couldn't count on it.

Salvage

for my mother, the girl from Avon

So many tales I should have fished from your depths,

stories of life by the sea, hurricanes rearranging your world.

The salty soup of raising brothers and sisters

because your own mother never woke up again.

A mother should be eternal.

How to exist without the loving gaze, the knowing eye?

Was the first new dress blue? What was the name of that dog?

The one you sneaked into the house,

a house of orphans saving scraps and feeding the pup at night,

covering his doggie noises with loud coughing.

And your first kiss?

Were you standing near the stove all your life for warmth?

So much mother from such an early age,

and then again mother to your own brooding line,

ushering us into flesh and blood and bone.

Did your own ma return to you, bringing you ashore?

Did you see her again, as I sometimes see you,

awash in a spray of salty stars?

The gate where the garden should be

is overgrown with weeds and wasted time.

I think of the untethered house, the one your aunt recounts,

your face floating in the upstairs window.

You could have drifted out to sea standing in your own bedroom,

but the winds calmed, waters receded in time,

and the house settled back on its cement haunches,

a little unsteady but safe,

with you sealed inside that great ark of memory.

Tell me, what was the chant or charm for ebb tides?

Edge of Morning

Birds begin their sharp notes before light.

The dream curls into its own ragged edges,

your mother's voice trails off.

The patter of rain becomes more insistent.

The sheets embroidered with roses replace

the room where you just sat with her

drinking bees in honeyed conversation.

All day you will try to recall the sweet vowels.

But time plays its sequence of pranks,

makes the body its puppet, its conquered.

The murmuring hum thrums through the day

still, with its wishing, with its whisper,

its unspoken desire:

the idea of not gone forever.

Personal Effects

I saved her dying nightgown as if a treasure,

stored in a chest deep in my closet.

The cheap nylon fabric, a wan blue,

has a small rust-hued smudge, a bloodstain

just where her hip might have curved.

My sisters and I, dividing her things,

lifted the gown to our faces, each in turn,

as if a ritual, a communion, her scent our host.

Why have I kept it all these years,

buried in that dark corner, shrouded

as memory, not memorial nor consigned

to thrift...why? Simply this—because,

because I could not keep her.

Hanging Out

It's what we did—

hide and seek in the hayloft,

cupping tadpoles in our palms,

watching them flit, throwing knives into a tree,

blade tip between thumb and forefinger,

the satisfying thunk of an on-target hit.

Do you want to hang out?

meant we're friends

let's do nothing together—it's better than alone,

meant rambling conversations,

meant paper airplanes, tomato sandwiches,

sneaking out after dark, meant the world to me.

I want to hang out again.

I want the gone world back.

Look, I found matches,

we could make a fire.

Middle School Love Lessons

for Gayle

1.

I ate strawberries from our garden,

my sticky fingers berry-stained by

those pocked red hearts,

grit-kissed, sun-warm.

It was a kind of love, requited

between heaven and earth, with me

centered between, weighing

hunger and its sating.

Strawberries red as valentine hearts

slipped into construction paper folders

pressed to an elementary school wall

on a Tuesday in February, pressed

like a girl to the seat on the back of the bus

by a boy, with other boys watching.

2.

Rural kids made their own Valentines,

Do you like me? Check yes or no.

Careful calligraphy, direct, aimed at the heart.

That's what we gave and got.

One X could send you skyward beaming,

or cast you so far down you could see

nothing but your own ragged shoes for days.

Supermarket strawberries are stripped

of their blood, no bloom on the tongue.

Sun-starved, a mockery of sweetness,

forced to grow red in transit.

3.

To make a heart out of paper,

fold the page down the middle,

cut out half of a heart. Be precise.

It must open out evenly to ever be whole.

As for strawberries, find them in season

where they grow, enjoy them under the sun,

out in the open.

Bon Voyage

"la mort serait un beau long voyage / death would be a long beautiful voyage"
Tristan Tzara from La Mort de Guillaume Apollinaire

I'm waving. I'm beside the ship about to sail.

I'm waving, and I'm singing *bon voyage, bon voyage*

because I want your trip to be beautiful:

bluebird skies, rain pattering musical notes,

an iridescent map of snail trails on stone,

honeysuckle, jasmine, magnolia dappled shade,

a long and welcome kiss, the fish slip into water,

floating under clouds that we name into things,

child at the breast, sailing on a bike through summer,

wood smoke, nights the moon illuminates...

What a sleek ship this is, like the skin of a shark,

or the furl of a wave heading ashore,

and you there with your hair young in the wind

laughing as if at the best joke, *bon voyage.*

II

A Small Village in France

"The past is a foreign country…" L. P. Hartley

Musical voices rise

to my room from the street below,

greeting, commenting on weather, calling dogs,

accents mingling with my dreams

in the un-shuttered, half-awake early hours.

A church bell tolls, sends me

to the small island of childhood, Sunday

worshippers walk the narrow lanes,

my stiff shoes and crinoline in solemn motion.

Mother took my hand along the way.

A chorus of mourning doves braids the trinity of time.

Cats snooze in window sills, hens peck at pebbles,

a phrase from Rilke crosses the border

into consciousness: *to neither quite belonging.*

Early Spring Aubade

Birds compete with chitters,

chirps, caws, trills,

a loud legion of Aves

to herald the sunrise.

Silence shrinks to the corners,

where my shoes

form a two step

beside crumpled clothes.

The demands of morning

are elemental and real.

The toilet down the corridor

a cold, necessary trip,

but tea will invite me to table,

bread for toast

butter, jam.

It will be enough.

Maybe that is the key

I've misplaced:

to find enough.

Enough light to see

without being blinded;

sing loud, without shouting;

a balance of hold and

release, a turn

of the corner.

Even empty palms,

cupped too long, fill

with a stone weight.

County Cork

What to make of such a place, what to make, make, make, taps the machine of making, the alphabet confined to manufacture meaning, make sense why don't you make sense? But what's to be made of this cobble, this clovered pasture, this bright air of water, what's to be made? I would fold down the limbs of this tree for a ladder if it could help us up to see better, or bring the sky level. The wind hollows and wolves at a window, a room rattles the door outside in. No one champions nature's clash. A woman passing yells, "pull yer head out of yer ass, man" and grasses spring from the ground, willing witnesses, applause. Cows low and look cow-eyed unknowing the predator is snapping a photo, cooing. The sheep are bucolic by the pub full of stew. There are fingers combing through hair as if an answer might be found there. What to make of such a place—the stout hearted, the fierce music impassively played, the cliff abyss, and all the while a green of things inexhaustible.

The Name of that Desire

It was, as they say, on the tip of my tongue

but that placement only led to more confusion,

a translation into a kind of longing

that signals loss in any language.

The wind was rearranging the trees

and carrying cotton to be caught in

webs, branches, still bodies of water—

this merging dance was part of the name.

The mad chatter of many birds, too,

was part—sibilant fragments,

throaty half syllables of reach and empty,

the last dream image dispersing to daylight.

Voice Lessons

The perfect correspondence between light and water—

bright ripples over the sea surface that still show

the bronze ribs of sand underneath.

I want to speak in natural elements just this way—

sounds combined by breath, like breaking

through the water's surface—that first gasp of air.

How were we before outcast, before other,

pulled so by the poor milked moon—so touchstone,

so lorn, full and crescent and gone.

Late Morning in Bed

Desire returns unexpectedly as I lie in bed on a sunny day.

Voices drift up from the courtyard below, the musical greetings,

gravel footsteps synched with a language I don't fully comprehend.

At first I only think how odd and funny, try to read, but the body,

well, it makes its demands. It must be given its due and

after all the sheets are so smooth and the reach not so far.

I stay discreetly under covers but the voices so near

make me feel on display, make me feel a flicker of wild,

make me feel oh *comment va dire* make me feel, make me feel

and I'm there. Then again, and just to be sated, again.

A woman's laugh rises up and some low throated reply.

Those flirts, and me lazing here now, wet hand and all.

Short Flight from a French Bike

I didn't tumble down a rabbit hole

to land safely on my feet.

I flew afield after the sharp drop,

to hit solid ground sprawling.

When I opened one eye,

there was a snail an inch away

waving moist tentacles.

Soon, there was a dog.

Its owner, the farmer, maybe,

warns it away from me.

I think *I need to get up.*

My left side did not agree.

My right side stayed silent.

OK? The man asks. *OK?*

Oui, OK. I stood on my right foot,

brushed some twigs from my hair.

Beau chien, I offer, in my miserable French.

Perhaps I should not be planted in his field?

Elle est ma fille. He shifts his eyes.

Ah, belle chien, I think I correct,

but my head still reels.

They continue down the lane.

I begin the short trek,

that redefines time,

rolling the wobbled wheels

in a squeaky metronome.

My new totem, the snail, inspires me,

slow, steady.

A million years later,

back in my rented room,

I curl into a goose down shell,

hoping escargot will not end up

on tonight's table.

Hair Fable

One day an ordinary girl became extraordinary by changing her hair. She was a brunette. Or a blond. She definitely wasn't a redhead because, as we know, she was ordinary. Her hair liked its new twists. It became musical, siren hair, jazz locks. People looked at her not only twice but with such sustained fascination, her hair noticed and decided to up the ante. Once her hair took over, no one could say for sure what would happen. One day, it became talons and snatched a small child off the pavement, or a poodle, depends on who tells the story. Some days, it became synchronized air swimmers performing miraculous routines of complex oxygen. If she crossed a street on those days, accidents would invariably occur. Some days, her hair was meteor and no one knew after she passed by why they had a sense of narrowly escaping death. Her hair knew. It liked its power. One day, she tried to tame it. It singed her hands. She never tried that again. On church days, her hair would be devilish, but when she danced wildly with an attractive man, her hair hung about demurely, frumpish as a spinster. Soon, she learned to just follow her hair. If it was wild, she was too. If it was a kite, she was a string. If it was birdsong, she was air. Her hair flew her around the small village, sometimes skyward, sometimes river skimming. Mothers tied scarves on their daughters, and smoothed down their own chignons.

They knew trouble when they saw it. Still, her hair captured every eye, even baby Rose, taking her first steps, stared up into a tree to see her tangled there. Maybe it was just the wind that blew Rose's crocheted cap right off her head and bubbled her with giggles. Maybe the gusts that rattled kitchen windows were no more forceful than they had ever been. Maybe the young girls only began to sneak out at night to see whether those were clouds across the moon or the streaming hair of an ordinary girl, just like them, who became extraordinary.

Wendy to the Lost Boys

I loved you all, my smelly tribe,

pen-knife to my heart: your needs and adoration,

your pre-pubescent lust that I see now

was just the cusp of your desire for me.

I welcomed your dirty finger-nail grasp,

your slack-jawed fascination

when I cast the tales that reeled you in.

I never minded how you scrambled to stand below me

when I climbed the tree house ladder.

I felt your eyes searing in, the inarticulate heat.

You were the best you were ever going to be

in the mute filth you called adventure,

sloth made into daring, random incoherent freedoms.

I found my need in yours.

You came night after night

in fine weather or rain, in the dank heat,

always wanting, never to be made whole,

and I gave. That was my role.

I was your Wendy.

for Toots with his dead mom and never a pop,

my shoulder a perfect fit for his hanging head

for Sly who needed a story, any story, as long as

it ended happily, the wished-for finale

for Tom who nuzzled with his eyes closed,

like a mole burrowing an underground maze

of blind possibility

for Billy who wanted to wear my panties

and I let him because why not?

Goose, gander and all.

And Peter. Well, about Peter, too little really could not be said.

It is the tribe that comes back to me at night now.

In all your collective singularity.

I'm not one for regret, especially now

as loss piles on loss.

So when your heads bob up in the wake

like buoys of clutch and release

I welcome you. We could have never

come so far, except together.

And, yes, my dears,

my lost ones,

I will walk the plank for you

one more time.

Outside the Metro

So many outstretched palms.

Those empty cups as I pass by,

an O of need and hunger,

an upturned hat beside a guitar with

only three strings left to strum.

Behind the one with dreads,

a siren wails, a babe without a bottle.

As I go by, I wish myself

invisible or earless, or better:

more prepared,

more providing.

I have no bread, no fish.

My jeans indict me,

my silk scarf knots my neck

in paisley judgement.

I wish I could conjure

the scent of jasmine, a bloom

to vanquish the stench of piss

overwhelming this ancient alley.

If only that coat of many

colors could drape us all,

cover the lot of us,

as we huddle together

remembering

how once we were

brothers.

The Day Began to be Sad

This day had no bread,

had only a hangover from a drunken argument

that was just a memory of no memory

(who said what? who turned out the light?)

It wants the ticket to backwards

to be again the happy night—

the dancing on the lawn, the starry hunt,

vinyl music, velvet grass,

pikes of laughter.

Sheets of rain gray over the scene.

A hundred years ago a child's incantation

worked its charm

over the rooftops of houses,

a ball could come back into play

Ollie Ollie oxen free,

but not today.

Today has gone moldy,

gone muddy, gone gone,

slid into a heap of regret.

No bread, and petals fall battered from the rose.

Three Cats + Booze = Jazz

Three cats prowled through an open door,

CeCe, Lion, and Green Man.

The room arched its back, the night

began to buzz, to jump and jive.

These cats wailed,

amped up the electricity, licked shadows

with bourbon bones and smoky spirits.

If ankles were lovers they uncrossed them,

made them starry, leafy, leaping

jitterbug twitchy.

The way cats do, they stayed or left

by their own design, springing impossibly up

to a rooftop or bridge or tobacco-coiled ruff.

These cats sharpen their claws on

repeated riffs before snaring the night's soft chest

or inviting lap to purr into, prize time.

Spang-a-lang. Bebop on down.

L'eglise de Marnay-sur-Seine

summer 2015

The church is locked.

Its imposing spire pierces the sky,

but the doors are sealed tight as tombs.

Its stone tower is bell-less this year.

The toll of centuries hushed,

concealed confessions,

songs stalled in every corner.

What voice was last heard here?

The widow at her ceaseless beads?

The repentant fornicator hoping not to beget?

The child who saw angels in your rosy window?

Are you solely relic now, a memorial

of bloody nails and wood,

from some forgotten age?

In a small town,

you are a grand monument,

like cemetery shrines, with their intricate

angels, crosses, scrolls, inscriptions.

Sculpted from those same stones,

you might be just another

marker of what has passed,

except for the long shadow you still cast.

Lady in Green and Gold

after Luis José Estremadoyro's painting
The Nightly Unfolding of Madame de Loynes

I coined my face for past and future purchase.

Was it wrong to materialize in such a way

the spirit that parted the veil for me,

the hand drawing aside

the green curtain of being?

The gold wrapping of gesture, the gaze

of generations, the secret smile

came to me easily as breath, as if

already existing before embodied.

What else was I to do with my waiting here?

My hand is always poised to bless

but also ringed with gold.

Wandering Père Lachaise

A village of the dead, *la cemetaire*,

elaborately sculpted stones

and some old tombs that look

as if the buried have busted out of them—

the liberated dead roaming

the cobbled pathways on air.

A crow lights on a sepulcher, oblivious

of how symbolic he looks to my human eye.

His flapping take off—the sound of souls

beating a retreat, but he merely seeks water.

Fresh, decayed, plastic—flowers of all sorts

are bunched by tombstones, a message

to those who can no longer be touched. Old

angers, joy, laughter, tears, love—how

long will they remain?

Celebrities here, still shining

in perfect death: flawless, slender, absent

even as some hearts grow fonder.

Saints, too, stamped by dying.

The dead are stars. They shine

a white gold light, bone enamel,

granite fame, the gravitas and ethereal

nature of their new roles—

an endless novena.

Rooftops

The rooftops are alight with sunset

they peak and flatten simultaneously.

They promise nothing.

The sky stretches past the rooftops

into infinity, into whatever eternity is.

Whatever it is, it is blue.

The rooftops wood and slate.

The rooftops plank and bird.

They are endless

outside the frame of this window.

They speak of other lives.

Some dive forward,

some retreat.

They converse in the beyond.

The rooftops plank and bird,

the rooftops blue and sunset.

Things Left Out in the Rain

The plastic table, its blue veneer puckering,

bottles, ashtray, unmatched shoes,

a book of poetry in French,

conversation about the lover,

a wish for bending time,

clothes on the line, dripping now,

lighter, some glasses ringed with wine,

that crazy laughter a little too loud,

a little too long, punctuated with a hiccup,

seat cushion, several sighs,

the ambiguous goodbye embrace.

III

Hungry People

Will eat anything, mother used to say.

I consider that as I eat top ramen with a corkscrew.

No fork in this dim, airless room.

Heart-starved, bleary, barren as a crone,

I shovel in noodles and try to remember

the girl from yesterday. Oh, she was fun.

She hitched up her skirt and mooned the sky,

pitched from volcanic tides, handy with a flip

off, belly full of laughter. That one.

Brokedown Palace Revisited

Against these eggshell walls

the blue plate of marriage smashed.

Kaleidoscopic shards predicted

the shattered détente with X.

Outside of these walls: torn maps,

liberty belle's crack is a chasm,

endless loop of towers falling,

red alert. Words full of air

break on deaf ears.

Broken: vows, chalice,

my metaphorical spine,

my actual right leg,

bridges, bonds, border-

worlds.

I'm drowning in a sad song

until the ancestral voice in my head

breaks into the brooding notes:

sit down & shut up

you ain't broke

til you can see the alphabet

in the dirt under your nails

and it spells home

Sparrow

Don't sing of regrets or none.

We note the categories, cages,

even nightingales can't neglect

this common scale, the open clef,

a wound.

We tried ascending/descending

but the fractured bones broke,

unmeasured lace splintering.

[wingspan of clipped fingernail moons/

planes on a collision course]

aversion, aggressive, aggrieved

those are the a's

B is for bird

but this is not an abecedary.

Not enough vowels,

emphatic consonants smash panes,

breast feathers lunge there,

end on pine needles,

around flowers no one names.

So much for the hero's journey.

I am aflame here

as in flame

there is no I.

Storm Diver

Shutters bang and doors slam. The day

tear-stained, a blurry mess.

Leave the hollow quarrel

echoing in the house, and let the rain

rain down on your briny face.

Let the wind bite your cheek.

Stay outside long enough, bootless,

to be made ragged by weather.

Notice how the tree trunks darken,

how their gnarled roots cleave the earth.

There will be bottles and beige rooms

to anesthetize your return, to absorb you.

Pillows of small talk, self-deception,

the plush of creature comforts to cushion

your inevitable return.

But just for now, allow the howling throat of wind

to swallow you, stripped down to your salt,

dive into the drenched wrack sealed inside

and plow under, into the green wave.

Leftovers

The refrigerator continues to leak

after clicking out translucent ice cubes.

Leftovers go to waste.

Who knows how to repair the uneven air?

The kitchen table has fewer things,

half-written notes, all in the same hand.

It floats in early evening when fading light

partially erases its legs.

At night, the neighbor's dog barks,

a frantic plea. I dream of wire cutters,

a midnight operation on the chain link fence,

her prison, in solitary moonlight.

Mornings when the sky begins to blue,

before daylight bleaches the dark corners,

I string together a necklace of memories,

moments of mingled laughter, when absence

was an abstract noun.

Ode to Sheets

I spread you over the bed,

so worn in places the light shines through,

once white, then eggshell or dun.

We drove against you in sweaty

clutches of desire, we fevered

and chilled on your cotton.

And, of course, we slept, snored,

drooled and catnapped on you.

You were the backdrop to our

ordinary drama: the fret of nightmares,

the haunt of 3 a.m. anxiety, the quarrel

that did not end with a kiss,

and the quiet travel to the otherworld

of novels, magazines, and dreams.

You came clean weekly,

fresh-scented Saturday afternoons,

you tempted us back to snuggle and cuddle.

The late afternoon sun on your expanse

offered a Renaissance of well-being.

You were a gift, a celebration of marriage.

You remained a gift of everyday comfort.

Thin as you got, you marked our time—

waning, like a hairline moving back,

or skin thinning towards transparency.

How many years you counted

our coupling and uncoupling, how many

before worn out, threadbare and exhausted,

you ended in the rag basket,

assigned to other uses, replaced

by those that come after.

Forgive Me

for plums and William Carlos Williams and that day

A bird etched an insistent V in the sky

that I took as a sign.

You wore a green coat

and I believed in the river

that moved us.

At the blink

of sun on curled water,

the ripple of branch snag,

a startled consonant of *now*,

I reached out my hand to you,

as if a fish had broken the surface to say

This hull I now call home.

Forgive me,

perhaps the gesture was too slight

even for such frail intent.

This is just to say:

Yes, I swallowed you with my eyes,

even as you rowed towards a different shore.

But, I, I was there to see that moment you turned

to cast your eyes, like much mended nets,

on me, then away again

to the sweep of river behind us.

The wind fractured with birdsong,

and the sky either threatened or promised,

we'll never know which.

River Analytics

The river is a nostalgic geometry,

an equation of time

with a common ratio of here and not here.

Solve for X. There is no Y.

The river curves toward infinity,

exponentially increased by hearts

pumped full of love and loss,

and tragicomic self-interest.

Observe. The constant is variable.

The function of water is to remember.

It ripples past a line of willows.

Listen to their sighing:

Recall a current of absolute value.

Garden Snake in a Fool's Paradise

He leaves you with nothing, not even

    the sticky illumination of a snail trail,

        iridescent glimmer of slow travel,

            no scent, no slow eroding musk or skunk,

                not even manure, webs, or hoof prints.

This garden snake is green, but leaves no green,

    even as he glissades through the weeds,

        he leaves no trace of color, not even clear memory

            of the quick thrill, the flash of slither,

                no recollection nor sweeping nostalgia for ritual or charm.

In the wake of his undulation, you stand stock still,

    and seek only a response, quite simply you seek to feel

        something, but this is the garden snake

            in your own fool's paradise, not perception.

            He leaves you with nothing.

Covenant

As we forgive those who trespass...

it's part of the bargain

it cannot be forgotten

that forgiven is a deal struck

without match, without lash,

without fist, instead the hand extended

to a drowning enemy

lest the death we wished for him occur.

Lessons from Genesis
for Kim Wyatt

"See how the bark whitens here," she says,

"that tells you it is a white, not red, fir."

I watch her teeth in smile,

how native to beauty.

I point at the plant by her feet.

"Stonecrop," she says.

I think *the red is trust in spring.*

She speaks a new world into being.

Riding a Bike at Dusk

The air an aviary of chitterings, cheeps,

the air a prism of mist on my face, scented

with dank green earth, rippled

by a quick startle of wings,

a woman's body moves through this space,

but a girl emerges from the green tunnel,

unconfined to now so that I am her again,

and her, then her.

The interminable longing to loft, to lift,

true as veins pulsing under skin, threading

past to future in this present moment.

As in dreams when the world reshapes,

this shift from one breath to another,

this merging of here and gone.

How open the heart is in transit,

how the body moves to reclaim itself

each instant.

The trees wave their wet leaves.

These are not tears.

Night Currents

At the bridge a train passes through my center,

a meteor splits the sky into two darknesses,

without direction a blue zipper grinds its teeth.

When the bike messenger came with our papers

we had to tell him he was centuries too late.

History had closed the book, the alphabet changed.

Now when the river eddies into noirish snakes,

we do not fear it. We still do not understand it,

but we care less and less. One day it will empty.